Forest Fun

Zoë Clarke

Quarto is the authority on a wide range of topics.

Quarto educates, entertains and enriches the lives of our readers—enthusiasts and lovers of hands-on living.

www.quartoknows.com

Author: Zoë Clarke
Series Editor: Joyce Bentley
Editor: Sasha Morton
Consultant: Helen Marron
Designer: Elaine Wilkinson

© 2019 Quarto Publishing plc

First published in 2019 by QED Publishing,
an imprint of The Quarto Group.
The Old Brewery, 6 Blundell Street,
London N7 9BH, United Kingdom.
T (0)20 7700 6700 F (0)20 7700 8066
www.QuartoKnows.com

A catalogue record for this book is available from the British Library.

ISBN 978-0-7112-4418-4

MIX
Paper from responsible sources
FSC® C001701

Manufactured in Shenzhen, China PP072019

9 8 7 6 5 4 3 2 1

Photo Acknowledgments

Shutterstock: front cover leonrwoods; back cover, p2 and 23 Triff; title page and p17t wavebreakmedia; p3 and 14-15 giuseppelombardo; p4-5 and 20 Smileus; p5 and 22 Pavel Kobysh; p6 Maxim Blinkov; p7t Andrei Zveaghintev; p7b Olga Koberidze; p8 samodelkin8; p9t Jiri Prochazka; p9b Sandra Standbridge; p10-11 and 20 Viktor Sergeevich; p11t Bruce MacQueen; p11b and 20 Jamie Hall; p12 and 20 Sergey Novikov; p14-15 Stratos Giannikos; p15 Shane Nixon; p16 Tsomka; p17b Enna8982; p18 Leszek Glasner; p19 and 20 Victoria43; p21 Olga Sapegina

Forest Fun

You can have lots of fun in the forest.

You can pick up pine cones.

You can jump in leaves.

Hop on to a log. Don't fall off!

Look for
big roots.

You can look for little bugs under logs and bark.

Some bugs have lots of legs.

Can you spot all of them?

Can you see a nest in the forest?

chicks

nest

Can you see a squirrel in the tree?

Badgers come out at night!

11

You can ride your bike in the forest.

Go on a zip wire and zoom between the trees!

13

Go up a tree. Don't go too high!

Look at a map to pick where to go next.

Make a den with big sticks and logs. Can you fit in it?

16

Put up a tent and camp in the forest.

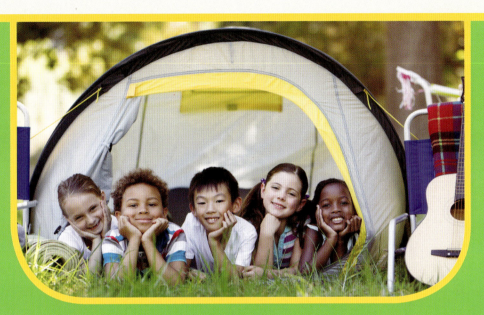

You can camp with your dogs too!

Take pictures of the forest.

Make pictures from leaves. Have fun!

Your Turn

Match it!

Follow the line from each picture
to read the word.

picture

bikes

badger

forest

chicks

Clap it!

Say the 'Match it!' words.
Clap and count
the syllables.

Sound it!

Sound out each of these words.

d ar k   l oo k   h igh   s t i ck s

Say it!

Read and say these words.

have   come   where   you   go

Spot it!

1. **Look at page 7.** Which word has a long **oo** sound?

2. **Look at page 8.** Which word has an **ar** sound?

Finish it!

Look back and find which word is missing.

1. **Page 5.** You can _____ up pine cones.

2. **Page 11.** _____ come out at night.

Count it!

1. **Page 4.** How many words are there in this sentence?

2. **Page 12.** Which word has six letters?

Sort it!

Sort the letters to spell a word.
Can you find the word in the book?

1 p j m u

2 ee r t

3 t t e n

4 b g u s

Do it!

Find four different types of leaves.
Draw around their shapes.
Can you find out which trees they come from?

Notes for Parents and Teachers

Children naturally practise their literacy skills as they discover the world around them. The topics in the **QED Essentials** series help children use these developing skills and broaden their knowledge and vocabulary. Once they have finished reading the text, encourage your child to demonstrate their understanding by having a go at the activities on pages 20–23.

Reading Tips

- Sit next to your child and let them turn the pages themselves.

- Look through the book before you start reading together. Discuss what you can see on the cover first.

- Encourage your child to use a finger to track the text as they read.

- Keep reading and talking sessions short and at a time that works for both of you. Try to make it a relaxing moment to share with your child.

- Prompt your child to use the picture clues to support their reading when they come across unfamiliar words.

- Give lots of praise as your child reads and return to the book as often as you can. Re-reading leads to greater confidence and fluency.

- Remind your child to use their letter sound knowledge to work out new words.

- Use the 'Your Turn' pages to practise reading new words and to encourage your child to talk about the text.

Can you see a nest in the forest?

chicks

Can you see a squirrel in the tree?

Short, decodable sentences repeat topic words and commonly used words

nest

Wide range of vocabulary to explore in context

Badgers come out at night!

Colourful photographs open up further discussion points

10

11